UTILIZING AI FOR PRODUCTIVITY

Utilizing AI for Productivity

Arnold Connor

Bald and Bonkers Network Academy

Disclaimer

This book has been written for information purposes only. Every effort has been made to make this book as complete and accurate as possible. However, there may be mistakes in typography or content. Additionally, this book provides information only up to the publishing date. Therefore, this book should be used as a guide, not as the ultimate source.
The purpose of this book is to educate. The author and the publisher do not warrant that the information contained in this book is fully complete and shall not be responsible for any errors or omissions. The author and publisher shall have neither liability nor responsibility to any person or entity with respect to any loss or damage caused or alleged to be caused directly or indirectly by this book.
This book offers information and is designed for educational purposes only. You should not rely on this information as a substitute for, nor does it replace, professional medical advice, diagnosis, or treatment.

Contents

Introduction

Artificial intelligence (AI) might seem like a concept straight out of a science fiction movie, but it has become a significant reality in the midst of the Digital Age. Contrary to popular fears, AI hasn't taken over the world and isn't likely to control everything. Instead, AI can be a powerful ally in overcoming procrastination and achieving seamless and effortless time management. This book will guide you on how to transform your productivity using AI tools.

Embracing AI in the Digital Age

As of 2023, AI can write content, create art, and engage in conversations. Additionally, it can automate mundane tasks, making them much easier to handle. Since we all have various priorities, leveraging AI can help manage tasks that otherwise feel tedious. This book will introduce you to the right AI tools, enabling you to prioritize daily tasks, delegate and schedule them efficiently. By the end of this book, you'll have a clear picture of how AI can enhance your life. You'll see AI as a beneficial tool rather than a threat, understanding its usefulness in many areas without replacing human capabilities.

How This Book Can Transform Your Workflow

Here's an overview of what you'll learn in this book, organized by chapter:

- **Chapter 1: The Basics of Productivity AI** - Before diving into specific tools, we'll discuss the fundamentals of AI in everyday applications. This chapter will help you identify your productivity and time management challenges.
- **Chapter 2: AI Tools for Efficient Time Management** - We'll explore tools like Google Calendar and how to integrate AI to smooth out any conflicts. You'll learn to harness AI for effective task management.
- **Chapter 3: Streamlining Communi-

cation and Collaboration - Discover how AI can enhance communication and collaboration, from emails to instant messages. We'll cover tools like Slack and their AI integrations.

- **Chapter 4: Project Management and Workflow Optimization** - Learn how to choose the best AI-enabled project management software and find workflow automation tools to streamline processes from start to finish.

- **Chapter 5: Content Creation and Management with AI** - Explore AI writing assistants and graphic design tools that simplify the content production process.

- **Chapter 6: Enhancing Personal Productivity** - Understand how AI can boost your personal productivity, including learning platforms for new skills and health apps for a healthier lifestyle.

Who is this book for?

This book is for anyone struggling with time

management and productivity or those looking to simplify life at home and work. If you're serious about improving your time management and automating tedious tasks with AI, this book is for you. It's designed to prompt action and can serve as a reference guide for troubleshooting your productivity plan using AI.

Now what...?

We hope this book offers valuable insights into AI and its potential to improve your productivity. Read each chapter carefully, take notes, and develop a plan to incorporate AI tools into your daily life, both personally and professionally. Ready to dive in? Turn the page to start with Chapter 1. See you there.

1

The Basics of Productivity AI

Understanding the Basics of Productivity AI

Understanding the fundamentals of productivity AI is crucial for long-term success, especially when selecting tools to streamline and optimize your tasks. AI has diverse applications, even requiring tailored prompts to meet individual needs and preferences. This chapter will cover essential aspects of AI in everyday tools and help you identify productivity challenges, enabling you to create effective solutions with AI. You will be amazed by how much AI can enhance your productivity while freeing up valuable time.

Understanding Artificial Intelligence in Everyday Tools

Artificial intelligence can seamlessly integrate with everyday tools to automate tasks that might otherwise seem tedious. Consider how we already interact with AI daily: asking Siri for information or instructing Alexa to perform tasks. AI is embedded in many applications, accessible through prompts or voice commands. Let's explore some common tools powered by AI.

Virtual Assistants

Virtual assistants like Siri, Alexa, and Google Assistant are powered by AI algorithms. These tools can set reminders, send messages, and provide real-time information such as weather and traffic updates. They also make personalized suggestions based on user behavior, such as recommending products on Amazon. This capability demonstrates AI's ability to understand and predict user preferences based on minimal behavioral data.

Smart Recommender Systems

Platforms like Netflix, Amazon Prime Video, and Spotify use AI-driven systems to recommend movies, TV shows, and music. These recommendations are based on user preferences and behavior, offering a personalized experience that saves time when deciding what to watch or listen to.

Language Processing Tools

AI-powered language processing tools, such as Grammarly, assist in improving writing by providing real-time suggestions for grammar, style, and tone. These tools are invaluable for content creation, email writing, and any task involving text, allowing for quick revisions before finalizing documents.

Identifying Productivity Challenges

Before leveraging AI for productivity, it is

essential to identify specific challenges you face. While these challenges vary from person to person, common productivity issues can often be addressed with AI. Here are some examples:

Time Management Issues

If you struggle to meet deadlines, miss appointments, or feel overwhelmed by a high volume of tasks, time management might be the issue. Set reminders to give yourself advanced notice of upcoming tasks, such as scheduling a reminder an hour before a meeting.

Lack of Focus

Difficulty concentrating, procrastinating, or getting easily distracted indicates a lack of focus. AI can help by managing distractions. For instance, instructing your virtual assistant to activate "Do Not Disturb" mode on your mobile device can minimize interruptions from notifications.

Ineffective Communication

Poor communication can impede project progress, causing misunderstandings, errors, and delays. AI tools can facilitate quick and clear messaging, ensuring that the right information reaches the right people efficiently.

Task Overload

Taking on too many tasks at once can lead to reduced productivity and burnout. Poor task management strategies may be to blame. AI tools can assist in planning and prioritizing tasks and delegating responsibilities to team members with the appropriate skills.

Final Thoughts

Now that you understand the basics of AI, you may realize how many AI tools you already use. AI proves its worth in enhancing productivity by performing tasks efficiently, whether through written prompts or voice commands. Identifying your productivity challenges is the first step; utilizing AI tools can help you address these issues and make your workflow smoother. Remember to stay on task and assess your workload to determine whether additional tasks can be managed or delegated effectively.

2

AI Tools for Efficient Time Management

Mastering Time Management with AI Tools

Time management is a crucial skill, yet not everyone excels at it naturally. Fortunately, with a basic understanding and the right AI tools, you can significantly improve your time management abilities. This chapter focuses on six different time and task management applications. These tools are valuable whether you are working solo or leading a team. Even if you are unfamiliar with some of these apps, they are worth exploring to enhance your productivity. Let's delve into these AI-integrated tools that can revolutionize your time management.

Intelligent Calendar Apps for Scheduling Mastery

One of the most effective ways to master your schedule is through intelligent calendar apps. These apps are ideal for meeting deadlines and scheduling appointments. Time management issues often stem from missing these critical elements. The following AI tools are excellent for scheduling:

Google Calendar with AI Integration

Google Calendar (calendar.google.com) incorporates AI to simplify scheduling. It suggests optimal meeting times, integrates with Gmail to create events, and adjusts events to resolve scheduling conflicts. Google Calendar makes scheduling straightforward with its AI capabilities.

Woven/Slack

Woven was a standalone calendar app that became part of Slack (slack.com) in 2021. Slack offers various AI-compatible calendar apps, providing an alternative to Google Calendar. If you seek a non-Google solution, Slack's extensive range of AI-integrated apps might be the right choice for you.

Clockwise

Clockwise (getclockwise.com) is a flexible calendar app that leverages AI to optimize your daily schedule. One standout feature is its ability to create blocks of focus time, minimizing interruptions. Clockwise also integrates with tools like Asana and Slack and offers statistics to help you set time management boundaries, improving your focus.

Task Management Software with AI Integration

Now that we've covered calendar apps, let's turn our attention to task management. Prioritizing tasks is essential for productivity. Keeping an organized list of tasks ensures you stay on track. Here are the top three AI-integrated task management software tools:

Todoist

Todoist (todoist.com) is a robust to-do list app. Its AI features help prioritize tasks, set intelligent reminders based on your habits, and provide personalized insights to achieve your productivity goals.

Any.do

Any.do is an excellent task management tool for individuals and teams. It utilizes AI to sort tasks and suggest times for task completion based on your behavior and existing calendar events. With its user-friendly design, Any.do is accessible on both desktop and mobile platforms.

Asana with AI Features

Asana (asana.com) has long been a top task management tool, now enhanced with AI. It identifies potential roadblocks, forecasts project timelines, and suggests workflow optimizations to ensure tasks are completed efficiently and on time. AI integration allows for smooth project progression, enabling teams to anticipate and address potential setbacks.

Considerations for Choosing AI Tools

Before selecting AI tools for time and task management, consider your specific challenges. Identify the issues you face and choose tools that best address these needs. Budget is another crucial factor; invest in tools that you can afford and that provide the desired functionality. Additionally, consider the features included in the tools. Do you need a calendar? Compatibility across devices and platforms is essential for seamless integration. Ensure the tools you choose are compatible with your preferred devices and platforms.

Final Thoughts

The six tools discussed in this chapter are

among the best available for managing time and tasks. They help eliminate poor time management and task overload, ensuring you meet deadlines and manage tasks efficiently. Choose tools that work best for you and your team. AI integration can significantly enhance productivity, making life easier for you and your project team.

3

——

Streamlining Communication and Collaboration

Effective communication is vital, whether with clients or project team members. Poor communication can result in misunderstandings, project failures, and significant setbacks. This chapter delves into the realm of AI-enhanced communication and collaboration tools designed to streamline workflows and enhance efficiency for entrepreneurs, solopreneurs, and remote workers worldwide.

We'll explore a variety of apps and tools

focused on email management, team collaboration, and project management. Additionally, we'll review case studies highlighting the effectiveness of these apps in real-world scenarios.

Email Management Apps with Smart Features

Email remains a cornerstone of communication, even in the era of advanced internet technologies. AI-enhanced email clients can ensure emails are written correctly, scheduled appropriately, and effectively managed. These clients can prioritize, sort, and manage emails, allowing you to focus on urgent messages while setting aside others for later review.

Case Studies

Spark

Spark (sparkmailapp.com) leverages AI to categorize emails by priority using its "Priority and Pin" function. It groups emails by sender, making organization straightforward. Features include marking emails as "done," setting emails aside for later, and scheduling email sends. Spark also includes a focus feature to minimize distractions, helping increase productivity and effective communication with team members and clients. The Gatekeeper feature aids in deciding which emails to accept or reject, and automatic reminders ensure timely email sends. Spark is compatible with various email platforms, including Google, Yahoo!, Outlook, iCloud, IMAP, and Exchange.

Astro/Slack

Astro, now part of Slack, was initially designed to manage inbox overload using an AI assistant. It allows users to manage emails via chatbot, unsubscribe from email threads, save important emails, and designate VIP contacts. Integrating with Slack, it enhances team communication and email management within the Slack environment.

Collaborative Platforms with AI Integration

Effective project collaboration requires platforms that facilitate smooth workflows. Slack and

Microsoft Teams are leading collaborative platforms that integrate AI to enhance communication and workflow automation.

Slack

Scheduler AI (https://slack.com/apps/A02GA0771T6-scheduler-ai) and Reclaim.ai (https://slack.com/apps/ARSJUP4R0-reclaimai) are two apps that utilize AI to simplify scheduling and task management within Slack. These apps allow for easy calendar invites, rescheduling, task management, and auto-syncing of Slack status with scheduled commitments, such as Zoom meetings.

AI-Enhanced Project Management Tools

Monday.com and Asana

Monday.com and Asana are premier project management tools that utilize AI to improve functionality.

Monday.com

Monday.com offers a comprehensive suite of AI-powered tools for product management, agenda creation, content creation, marketing, and human resources. AI can break projects into manageable tasks, create meeting agendas from prompts, and rephrase messages to improve communication.

Asana

Asana integrates AI to optimize workflows, identify potential roadblocks, and facilitate seamless communication through natural language queries. It offers smart summaries of tasks, conversations, and comments, making project management more organized and efficient.

Automated Transcription and Meeting Summarization Tools

Automated transcription and meeting summarization tools capture every word spoken during meetings, ensuring you don't miss critical information. **Otter.ai** is a notable tool in this category, providing real-time meeting transcripts, allowing for comments and highlights, and integrating with platforms like Zoom, Google Meet, and Microsoft Teams. Live summaries ensure you capture essential points in real-time, aiding in informed decision-making.

Final Thoughts

AI can significantly enhance communication and collaboration, making team projects streamlined and efficient. It facilitates seamless communication, efficient email management, and effective task planning. AI-driven tools can act as personal assistants, providing critical information to aid decision-making for entrepreneurs and solopreneurs.

AI not only excels in time and task management but also in ensuring communication clarity and collaboration efficiency. By integrating these tools, you can improve productivity, streamline workflows, and achieve better project outcomes.

4

Project Management and Workflow Optimization

Effective project management and smooth workflow are essential for the success of any project. Ensuring that your project proceeds without hitches and that your workflow remains seamless is critical. This chapter explores how AI can enhance both project management and workflow optimization.

In the previous chapter, we touched on major players in project management like Asana, Monday.com, and Slack. With AI integration, these tools have gained remarkable capabilities, essentially giving them the "superpowers" needed to elevate productivity.

We will guide you through selecting the right AI-enabled project management software, providing a comprehensive list of considerations. Additionally, we will delve into workflow automation, ensuring your daily operations are streamlined.

Let's begin by exploring the essentials to find the best tools for your needs.

Selecting AI-Enabled Project Management Software

Choosing the right AI-enabled project management software requires careful consideration of several factors. Here is a detailed list of criteria to help you make an informed decision:

Integration with Existing Platforms

Ensure the software integrates seamlessly with platforms you already use, such as Google Drive, Microsoft Teams, Slack, and other CRMs, collaboration, or communication tools. Compatibility with your current infrastructure will enhance efficiency and reduce the learning curve.

Operating System Compatibility

Select software compatible with your operating systems, such as Windows, iOS, Android, or macOS. Verify that mobile applications, if available, are compatible with your devices to ensure accessibility on the go.

User-Friendly Interface

A user-friendly interface is crucial for ease of use by you and your team. The software should facilitate intuitive navigation and functionality, allowing all team members to perform their tasks without unnecessary complexity.

Customization Options

Opt for software that allows customization to fit your specific project management needs. This includes customizable dashboards and workflows, enabling you to tailor the software to your processes from start to finish.

AI Capabilities

AI capabilities are central to the software's value. Look for features such as task automation, forecasting, conflict detection, and intelligent suggestions. These capabilities will streamline operations, saving time and effort.

Data Security and Privacy

Security is paramount. Ensure the software offers robust data protection measures, including encryption and secure authentication. This is especially critical if you handle sensitive data.

Collaboration Features

Collaboration features are vital for team-based

projects. Look for real-time commenting, editing, and notifications to facilitate seamless communication and collaboration among team members.

Reporting and Analytics

The software should provide robust reporting and analytics features. These tools will help you track project progress, measure time savings from automation, and make informed decisions based on data-driven insights.

Mobile Accessibility

In today's digital age, mobile accessibility is essential. Choose software that offers mobile apps or responsive web pages, allowing you to manage projects from anywhere, at any time.

Budget

Budget is an important consideration. While cost is a factor, prioritize software that offers the best quality, performance, and features within your budget. Ensure that your most critical needs are met without compromising on quality.

Workflow Automation Tools for Streamlined Operations

Selecting workflow automation tools involves similar considerations. The goal is to find tools that ensure your team stays on track and operations run smoothly. Different tools serve various purposes, and it's essential to choose those that align with your specific business goals.

For instance, you might need a workflow automation tool for managing sales teams, monitoring projects, or facilitating communication. Ensure the tool can detect workflow conflicts when adding new tasks and is easy to use, minimizing the time spent on setup and training.

Here are a few recommended workflow automation tools:

- **Zapier (https://zapier.com/):** Automates tasks by connecting your apps and services, creating workflows that handle repetitive tasks.

- **Nintex (https://www.nintex.com/process-automation/workflow-automation):** Offers advanced workflow automation capabilities, ideal for complex processes.
- **Taskade (https://www.taskade.com/):** Provides a versatile platform for managing tasks, projects, and collaborations with AI-enhanced features.

Final Thoughts

Selecting the right AI-enabled project management and workflow optimization tools can be challenging, but this chapter aims to guide you in making the best choice. AI has significantly enhanced the capabilities of popular productivity tools like Zoom, Asana, and Slack, making them more powerful and efficient.

Investing in the right tools tailored to your needs will yield significant benefits, streamlining your workflow and enhancing project management.

While budget constraints may influence your selection, prioritize features and performance to find the best fit for your business and team projects.

5

Content Creation and Management with AI

The capabilities of AI in content creation and management are incredibly advanced. While this book wasn't written using AI tools, it's important to recognize how these technologies can significantly enhance marketing strategies for businesses. Well-crafted blog posts continue to attract traffic and potential customers. This chapter explores various AI-powered content creation and management tools, as well as popular graphic design tools with AI capabilities, to help you elevate your content production.

AI Writing Assistants for Enhanced Content Production

AI writing tools, powered by large language models (LLMs) such as Claude and GPT-3.5/4, offer user-friendly interfaces that simplify content creation. By providing specific prompts, these tools can generate high-quality content quickly. Here are some notable AI writing assistants:

- **Zimmwriter**: Ideal for creating SEO content for blogs, Zimmwriter's bulk blog writing feature allows you to produce up to 70,000 words of content with one click. It's available via a monthly subscription or a lifetime deal, although the latter may no longer be available after January 2024. This tool is perfect for efficiently generating multiple blog posts, saving significant time in the content creation process.

- **Copy.ai**: This tool excels in generating various types of marketing content, from ads to emails. Copy.ai simplifies the process of creating high-quality marketing materials, making it an excellent choice for businesses looking to enhance their marketing strategies.

- **Jasper**: Jasper is a powerful AI content creator suitable for large teams and solo entrepreneurs alike. It can generate image prompts, product descriptions, content summaries, and more. Jasper learns and adapts to your style, making it a versatile tool for diverse content needs.

- **ChatGPT**: Popular since late 2022, ChatGPT offers an affordable alternative to more sophisticated AI tools. Its free version, along with a premium option, makes it accessible for generating content and overcoming writer's block. Users can create custom prompts to produce tailored content efficiently.

Graphic Design Tools with AI Capabilities

AI has also revolutionized graphic design, making the creation of visual content more efficient and less time-consuming. Here are some top graphic design tools with AI features:

- **Jasper**: In addition to its writing capabilities, Jasper can generate unique, high-resolution images based on user prompts. This dual functionality makes it a valuable tool for creating both written and visual content.

- **Canva**: Canva's AI image generator allows users to create images from words and phrases for free. With additional filters and effects, you can enhance these images to fit your needs perfectly, without incurring extra costs.

- **DALL-E 2**: Developed by OpenAI, DALL-E 2 is renowned for creating high-quality images using natural language prompts. Users can generate multiple images, experimenting with textures, reflections, and other details to achieve the desired visual content.

Final Thoughts

AI-powered content creation tools, whether for text or images, are remarkably effective and continually improving. These tools are especially beneficial for entrepreneurs aiming to produce blog content, marketing materials, or visually appealing images quickly and efficiently. By selecting the right tools that align with your specific needs and preferences, you can streamline your content creation process, leveraging AI to create impactful and engaging content with just a few well-chosen words.

6

Enhancing Personal Productivity

In this final chapter, we shift our focus from the professional environment to personal productivity. While we have explored content creation, project management, and various other business-related topics, it's important to acknowledge that AI tools can significantly benefit personal development and well-being as well. This chapter will cover AI-powered learning platforms for skill development and health and wellness apps that incorporate AI features to help you maintain a healthy lifestyle.

Personalized AI Learning Platforms for Skill Development

AI learning platforms offer numerous benefits for skill development, including automating tasks, creating personalized learning experiences, and providing course recommendations based on your interests. Here are some notable platforms:

- **Teachable** (https://teachable.com/): Teachable is a well-established online course platform that has integrated AI to enhance curriculum creation. It offers features such as a quiz generator, subtitles and translations, and a summary generator, making course building more efficient. Whether you are creating or taking a course, Teachable's AI capabilities can streamline the learning process.

- **Memrise** (https://www.memrise.com/): Memrise is an AI-powered language learning platform that offers nearly two dozen languages in a gamified format. It includes an AI chatbot tutor to help you practice and improve your language skills through interactive conversations, making language learning more engaging and effective.

- **360 Learning** (https://360learning.com/): This platform provides personalized learning recommendations based on your behavior and training history. It also allows users to create their own courses. AI tools like Jasper and ChatGPT can be used to generate course content quickly, enabling course creators to provide customized learning experiences and allowing students to follow up with additional courses based on their learning progress.

Health and Wellness Apps with AI Features

Maintaining both physical and mental health is crucial, and AI-powered apps can help you track and improve your well-being. Here are some of the top health and wellness apps that incorporate AI features:

- **EvolveAI** (https://www.evolveai.app/):

EvolveAI functions as a personal trainer, offering personalized workout plans, dietary advice, and daily progress check-ins. It utilizes voice-to-text technology to help you track your fitness progress effortlessly, making it easier to meet your health goals.

- **Fitbod** (https://fitbod.me/): Fitbod is another excellent fitness app that tracks your progress based on muscle fatigue from previous workouts. This feature helps prevent injuries by ensuring you choose appropriate exercises. Fitbod is compatible with AI wearables such as Fitbit and Apple Health, enhancing its tracking capabilities.

- **Wysa** (https://www.wysa.com/): Wysa focuses on mental health by combining AI with human coaching. It provides mood tracking, positive thinking exercises, and support for mental health issues. Wysa is a valuable tool for both personal use and for supporting team members in a work environment, helping to maintain overall mental well-being.

Final Thoughts

AI is a powerful tool for enhancing personal productivity, skill development, and health management. Many productivity apps used in the office can also be adapted for personal use, allowing you to create checklists for daily routines, track dietary and fitness habits, and support mental well-being.

It's important to remember that AI does not replace emergency medical assistance. In case of severe health or mental health crises, always seek appropriate emergency help. However, for day-to-day health tracking and personal development, AI can be a valuable resource, helping you to take better care of yourself and optimize your productivity.

Conclusion

Thank you for taking the time to read this book and integrating AI into your personal and professional life. By now, you have gained valuable skills and insights into using AI tools to enhance productivity. Let's recap the key strategies and tools discussed throughout the book to ensure you can fully leverage AI in your daily activities.

Recap of Key Strategies and Tools

AI offers a multitude of capabilities to improve efficiency and effectiveness in various tasks. Here are some essential activities and corresponding AI tools to help you get the job done:

- **Virtual Assistants**: AI-powered virtual assistants can create reminders, provide news reports, weather updates, and traffic information using voice commands. These assistants, like Amazon's Alexa and Google

Assistant, are excellent for handling basic tasks and requests.

- **Time Management**: Scheduling appointments and meetings is simplified with AI prompts, ensuring you are always on time. Tools like Google Calendar utilize AI to manage your schedule and can even reschedule appointments when necessary.

- **Task Management**: AI can help you plan and prioritize tasks or delegate them to team members. Tools such as Slack and Microsoft Teams facilitate efficient task management, ensuring that the right tasks are assigned to the right people.

- **Effective Communication**: AI can assist in quickly drafting emails or messages, either through typing or voice commands. This feature ensures clear and effective communication within your team, saving time and enhancing productivity.

- **Project Management**: AI streamlines project management by delegating tasks based on team members' skill sets. Tools like Asana and Monday.com allow you to manage projects smoothly, reducing setbacks and improving team collaboration.

- **Content Creation and Management**: AI can generate written and visual content rapidly. Tools like DALL-E and Jasper enable you to create content tailored to your audience, whether for marketing purposes or generating awareness.

- **Personal Development**: AI can support your physical and mental health by tracking fitness and diet goals. Numerous AI-powered apps help you maintain and achieve your health objectives, motivating you to keep progressing.

Taking the Next Steps in Your AI Productivity Journey

As you conclude your journey through this book, it's time to chart your next steps in maximizing AI for productivity. Begin by revisiting the first chapter to identify your specific productivity challenges. Once you have a clear understanding of these challenges, explore AI apps that address them effectively.

Invest time in learning how to use these apps, as most are user-friendly and designed for easy adoption. Ensure that the apps you choose align with your critical needs, preferences, and budget.

We hope you have found this book insightful and beneficial. If you enjoyed reading it, please consider leaving a review. Thank you once again for reading, and we wish you the best in your AI productivity journey. And don't be afraidto do your own research to find better alternatives than what was suggested in these pages! Technology already was moving at a faster pace than most people could comprehend, the integration of AI will only make things faster and more accessible!

CHECKLIST

Automate Intelligently:

- **Identify Repetitive Tasks**: Determine tasks in your workflow that are repetitive and predictable.
- **Utilize AI Automation Tools**: Choose AI tools that seamlessly integrate with your existing processes.
- **Measure Efficiency Gains**: Track and evaluate the impact of automation on task completion times and overall productivity.

Make Smarter Decisions:

- **Understand AI in Decision-Making**: Learn how AI processes data to assist in making informed decisions.
- **Explore Decision Support Tools**: Investigate tools designed to enhance your decision-making process.
- **Adopt AI for Strategic Planning**: Use

AI for data analysis to make well-informed strategic decisions, even in tough situations.

Personalize Learning and Skills:

- **Set Learning Goals**: Identify your learning objectives and areas for skill development.
- **Use Adaptive Learning Platforms**: Engage with platforms that offer personalized content, allowing you to learn at your own pace.
- **Commit to Continuous Learning**: Leverage AI for ongoing skill enhancement and personal development.

Collaborate Effectively with AI:

- **Explore Collaboration Tools**: Find AI tools that enhance communication and project management.
- **Integrate Virtual Assistants**: Use virtual assistants to streamline coordination and information retrieval.
- **Optimize Teamwork**: Utilize AI tools to

reduce communication barriers and optimize task allocation, and regularly review available analytics.

Harness AI-Driven Insights for Strategy:

- **Acknowledge AI's Strategic Role**: Understand AI's capabilities in providing actionable insights for strategic planning.
- **Learn from Industry Examples**: Study how your industry leverages AI-driven insights for strategic decisions.
- **Address Ethical Considerations**: Develop strategies to integrate AI ethically, ensuring data privacy and compliance with regulations.

Navigate Challenges Responsibly:

- **Address Common Concerns**: Discuss job displacement, data security, and ethical implications with your team.
- **Implement Ethical Guidelines**: Establish

transparency measures to build trust in AI processes within your business.
- **Use AI Responsibly**: Prioritize employee training and data governance to ensure proper and ethical use of AI tools.

Commit to Continuous Learning:

- **Stay Informed About AI Advancements**: Keep up-to-date with AI developments and trends relevant to your field.
- **Engage in Skill-Building**: Participate in training programs to enhance your understanding of AI applications in your industry.
- **Collaborate and Share Knowledge**: Share your AI insights and knowledge with team members, colleagues, and network connections.

Embrace a Collaborative Approach:

- **Encourage Cross-Functional Collaboration**: Promote collaboration between different departments to maximize AI's impact.

- **Facilitate Open Communication**: Ensure clear communication channels regarding AI initiatives and their potential impact on your organization.
- **Cultivate a Collaborative Culture**: Build an organization that values and embraces AI's potential.

Additional Points:

- **Reap the Rewards of AI Integration**: Witness how AI can improve efficiency, decision-making, and overall productivity.
- **Address AI Challenges Responsibly**: Identify and address concerns about AI while adopting ethical guidelines.
- **Identify Useful Tools**: Determine which AI tools will address your productivity challenges.
- **Test and Evaluate Tools**: Try different AI tools that fit your budget and critical needs, utilizing free trials where available.